The Life and Work of
Paul Klee

Sean Connolly

Heinemann LIBRARY

www.heinemann.co.uk/library
Visit our website to find out more information about **Heinemann Library** books.

To order:
☎ Phone 44 (0) 1865 888066
▤ Send a fax to 44 (0) 1865 314091
▣ Visit the Heinemann Bookshop at www.heinemann.co.uk/library to browse our catalogue and order online.

First published in Great Britain by Heinemann Library, Halley Court, Jordan Hill, Oxford OX2 8EJ, part of Harcourt Education.
Heinemann is a registered trademark of Harcourt Education Ltd.

© Harcourt Education Ltd 2000, 2006
Second edition first published in paperback in 2007
The moral right of the proprietor has been asserted.

Editorial: Clare Lewis
Design: Jo Hinton-Malivoire and Q2A Creative
Illustrations by Sally Barton
Production: Helen McCreath

Printed and bound in China by South China Printing Company

13 digit ISBN 978 0 431 09890 6 (hardback)
10 09 08 07 06
10 9 8 7 6 5 4 3 2 1

13 digit ISBN 978 0 431 10437 9 (paperback)
11 10 09 08 07
10 9 8 7 6 5 4 3 2 1

British Library Cataloguing in Publication Data
Connolly, Sean
The Life and Work of: Paul Klee - 2nd edition
759.9'494
A full catalogue record for this book is available from the British Library.

Acknowledgements
The publishers would like to thank the following for permission to reproduce photographs:
AKG Photo, pp. 4, 10, 22, 24 Paul-Klee-Stiftung, Kunstmuseum, Bern/L Moillet, p.20. Fotopress/Walter Henggeler, p. 28;Page 5, Paul Klee *Familienspaziergang, 1930*, 264, Credit: Paul-Klee-Stiftung, Kunstmuseum, Bern. Page 7, Paul Klee *Dünen landschaft*, 19213, 139, Credit: Paul-Klee-Stiftung, Kunstmuseum, Bern. Page 9, Paul Klee *Schadau*, 1895/96, Credit: Paul-Klee-Stiftung, Kunstmuseum, Bern. Page 11, Paul Klee Siebzehn, irr. 1923, Credit: Oeffentliche Kunstsammlung Kupferstichkabinett, Basel. Page 13, Paul Klee *Meine Bude*, 1896, Credit: Paul-Klee-Stiftung, Kunstmuseum, Bern. Page 15, Paul Klee *Lily*, 1905, 32, Credit: Paul-Klee-Stiftung, Kunstmuseum, Bern. Page 17, Paul Klee, *Candide 7. Capitel "Il lève le voile d'une main timide"* 1911, 63, Credit: Paul-Klee-Stiftung, Kunstmuseum, Bern. Page 19, Paul Klee *Mädchen mit Krügen*, Credit: Paul-Klee-Stiftung, Kunstmuseum, Bern. Page 21, Paul Klee *Rote und Weisse Kuppeln*, 1914, 45, Credit: AKG Photo. Page 23, Paul Klee *Einst dem Grau der Nacht enttaucht…*, 1918, 17, Credit: Paul-Klee-Stiftung, Kunstmuseum, Bern. Page 25, Paul Klee *Plan einer garten-architektur, 1920*, 214, Credit: Bridgeman Art Library. Page 27, Paul Klee *Polyphon gefasstes Weiss, 1930*, 140(x10), Credit: Paul-Klee-Stiftung, Kunstmuseum, Bern. Page 29, Paul Klee *TOD und FEUER, 1940*, 332 (G 12), Credit: Paul-Klee-Stiftung, Kunstmuseum, Bern.

Cover photograph: *Ueberschach*, 1937, 141 (R 1), Super Chess, 120 x 110 cm, Olfarbe auf Jute auf Keilrahmen by Paul Klee, reproduced with permission of Rahmenleisten Kunsthaus Zurich.

The publishers would like to thank Nancy Harris for her assistance in the preparation of this book.

Some words in the book are bold, **like this**. You can find out what they mean by looking in the Glossary.

Contents

Who was Paul Klee?

Paul Klee was a Swiss painter and **graphic artist**. He liked to make very colourful paintings. His pictures make people think of music and dreams.

Paul kept a sense of fun in his paintings.
This picture shows how he liked to "take
a line for a walk".

Early years

Paul Klee was born on 18 December 1879 near the city of Berne in Switzerland. His family loved music. Paul learned to play the violin when he was seven years old.

1923 139 Dünen landschaft

Paul's uncle Ernst had a café. Paul liked
to look at the patterns on the tablecloths
there. This painting was made in 1923. It
shows Paul was still interested in patterns.

School days

Paul went to school in Berne. He still enjoyed music. He joined the Berne **orchestra** when he was only 10 years old.

Paul also began to enjoy drawing pictures. He filled his school notebooks with drawings and designs. He tried to show his love of music and poetry in his paintings.

The move to Germany

Paul left school when he was 19. He moved to Munich, Germany. There he began to **study** drawing and painting. Magazines like this one helped him to think of funny ideas.

Paul had a good sense of fun. He made
this picture in 1923. He was 44 years old.
It shows some interesting faces.

Learning to paint

In 1901
Paul **studied**
paintings in
Italy. He then
returned
to his family in
Berne. There
he **practised**
his own art and
tried out many
different ideas.

Most of Paul's works were drawings or **etchings**. This drawing of his bedroom shows how well Paul could draw.

A growing family

In 1906 Paul married Lily Stumpf. Their son Felix was born a year later. Lily earned money by playing piano **concerts**. Paul worked at home.

This is a painting of Lily. Paul **exhibited** some of his pictures in 1906. He became better known after the exhibition.

Public success

Paul's first one-man **exhibition** was in Berne in 1910. It was a great success. The same exhibition was then shown in other Swiss cities.

Paul's pictures were black and white. He used an ink pen and drew on white paper. This picture was used in a book.

A friendly welcome

Paul became friends with two other artists, August Macke and Wassily Kandinsky. Paul joined their group of **expressionist** artists. The group was called *Der Blaue Reiter* (*The Blue Rider*).

Paul also liked the work of other artists. He painted this picture in 1910. It looks like a painting by an artist called Paul Cézanne.

Colour takes hold

In 1914 Paul and August Macke visited Tunisia in Africa. Paul loved the bright light and colours there. He decided to stop using just black and white in his pictures.

The coloured squares in this painting look like the **mosaics** Paul saw in Tunisia. Mosaics are pictures made out of square coloured stones.

Rote u. weisse Kuppeln 1914.45

New directions

Paul was happy painting in many colours. He felt free to try some other new ideas. He started putting letters and numbers in his pictures.

Paul thought numbers and letters made people think of words and dreams. Paul felt he was making a new **language** in his pictures.

Time as a teacher

In 1920 Paul became a teacher at the
Bauhaus. This was the most famous art
school in Germany. Paul taught there
until 1931.

Paul's pictures show what he taught at the Bauhaus. He taught students that an artist is like a tree trunk. The branches are the thoughts he shows in his pictures.

Escape from Germany

A new **government**, called the **Nazis**, took power in Germany. They did not like Paul's pictures or those of many other artists. In 1933 Paul had to move to Switzerland.

The Nazis wanted pictures to look like real things. Paul did not agree. He used his colours and lines to make people think for themselves.

Illness and death

Paul caught a disease when he was 56 years old. He never got better. He still painted but he was always in pain. Paul died on 29 June 1940. He was 61 years old.

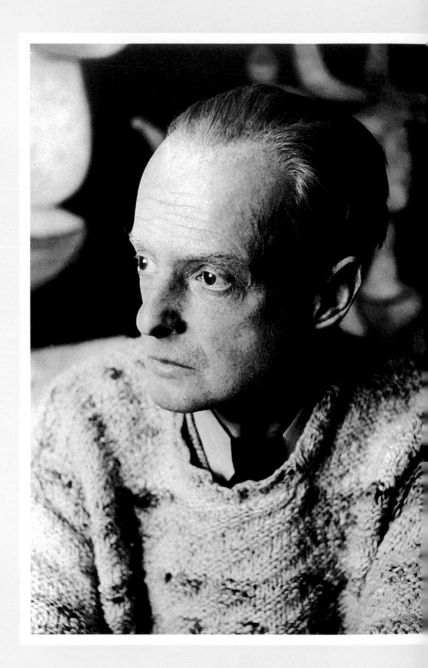

Paul's illness made him think about
death. His pictures became darker. Thick
black lines replaced the bright colours he
used when he was well.

Timeline

1879   Paul Klee is born near Berne, Switzerland on 18 December.

1886   Paul begins to **study** the violin.

1889   Paul joins Berne Municipal **Orchestra**.

1898   Paul leaves school and moves to Munich, Germany.

1906   Paul marries Lily Stumpf and has **etchings exhibited**.
            The artist Paul Cézanne dies.

1910   Paul has successful exhibitions in Switzerland.

1911   Paul joins *Der Blaue Reiter* group of **expressionist** artists.

1914   Paul visits Tunisia and decides to fill his pictures with colour.

1914–18   The First World War.

1920–31   Paul teaches at the famous Bauhaus art school in Germany.

1933   Paul is forced to leave Germany and go to Switzerland.

1935   Paul begins a long illness.

1939   The Second World War begins in Europe.

1940   Paul dies in Muralto, Switzerland on 29 June.

Glossary

concert playing music in public

etching picture made by drawing on a metal plate and then printing it

exhibit to show and sell works of art in public

expressionist type of art that changes the way things look to show feelings

government group of people who rule a country

graphic artist someone who makes pictures to print

language way of passing on ideas to other people

mosaic pattern of coloured stone used to make a picture

Nazi short name for the National Socialist German Workers' Party

orchestra group of musicians who play concerts in public

practise keep trying to do something to get better at it

study learn about a subject

More books to read

The Children's Book of Art, Rosie Dickens (Usborne Publishing, 2005)

More paintings to see

Comedy, Paul Klee, Tate Gallery, London

Seaside Resort in the South of Francc, Paul Klee, Tate Gallery, London

Index